W9-BQL-752

The Wild World of Animals

Manatees

Peaceful Plant-Eaters

by Adele D. Richardson

Consultant:
Nancy Sadusky
Communications Director
Save the Manatee Club

Bridgestone Books
an imprint of Capstone Press
Mankato, Minnesota

Bridgestone Books are published by Capstone Press
151 Good Counsel Drive, P.O. Box 669, Mankato, Minnesota 56002
http://www.capstone-press.com

Library of Congress Cataloging-in-Publication Data
Richardson, Adele, 1966–
    Manatees: peaceful plant-eaters/by Adele D. Richardson.
    p.cm. — (Wild world of animals)
    Summary: An introduction to the physical characteristics, behavior, various types, life cycle, and habitat of manatees, endangered marine animals that can live up to sixty years.
    Includes bibliographical references (p.24) and index.
    ISBN 0-7368-1395-0 (hardcover)
1. Manatees—Juvenile literature. [1. Manatees. 2. Endangered species.] I. Title. II. Series.
QL737.S63 R53 2003
599.55—dc21   2002000082

Editorial Credits
Heather Adamson, editor; Karen Risch, product planning editor; Linda Clavel, designer
    and illustrator; Kelly Garvin, photo researcher

Photo Credits
Bruce Coleman Inc., cover; Colla-V&W, 4, 16; Avampini-V&W, 6, 8
Digital Stock (texture), cover, 2, 3, 6, 8, 10, 18, 22, 23, 24
Doug Perrine/Seapics.com, 14
Fred Bavendam/Minden Pictures, 10
Fred Breeland, 20
U.S. Fish and Wildlife Service/Galen Rathburn, 1
USGS-Florida Caribbean Science Center, 18
William Munoz, 12

1 2 3 4 5 6 07 06 05 04 03 02

Table of Contents

eye

nostril

mouth

flippers

tail

4

Manatees

Manatees are large marine animals. They have two flippers and a flat tail shaped like a paddle. Manatees are gray. They usually grow to be about 10 feet (3 meters) long. They weigh about 1,200 pounds (544 kilograms).

marine

from the sea

Manatees are relatives of elephants. Some manatees have "toenails" on their flippers. They look like the toenails on elephant feet.

Manatees Are Mammals

Manatees are mammals. They are warm-blooded and have a backbone. Female manatees feed milk to their young. Manatees swim to the surface of the water to breathe air. Manatees breathe through two nostrils that close underwater.

nostril

an opening in the nose used for breathing and smelling

FUN FACTS

Manatees usually swim 3 to 5 miles (5 to 8 kilometers) per hour. They can swim at speeds of 20 miles (32 kilometers) per hour for short distances.

A Manatee's Habitat

A manatee's habitat is fresh or salt water. They live in the waters of West Africa, South America, Central America, and parts of the United States. The water is warmer than 70 degrees Fahrenheit (21 degrees Celsius). It is less than 15 feet (5 meters) deep.

habitat
the place where an animal lives

Manatees also are called sea cows.

What Do Manatees Eat?

Manatees are herbivores. They eat mostly plants. Manatees sometimes swallow small sea animals caught in the plants. They spend six to eight hours eating every day. Some manatees can eat up to 150 pounds (68 kilograms) of food in one day.

Manatee Teeth

Manatees have flat teeth called molars in the back of their mouths. The molars wear down from chewing. Manatees' worn teeth move forward in their mouths. New teeth grow in back. The worn teeth then fall out. Manatees grow new teeth their whole lives.

worn
run down from use

Mating and Birth

Female manatees produce a scent when they are ready to mate. Males follow the scent to find a female manatee. Several males mate with each female. The female gives birth to one young about a year later.

scent
the odor or smell of something

Manatee Calves

Young manatees are called calves. They weigh between 60 and 70 pounds (27 and 32 kilograms) at birth. Calves stay with their mothers for up to two years. Scientists think that manatees can live to be 60 years old.

Predators

Manatees have no natural predators. Only people harm manatees. Speeding boats often hit manatees. The manatees cannot move out of the way fast enough. The boats' propellers cut into their skin. These cuts can kill manatees or leave them with white scars.

propeller
a spinning blade
on a motor

Manatees and People

Manatees are endangered animals. Many people work to help manatees. Some groups care for hurt manatees. People in Florida put speed limits in places where manatees live. People must drive boats slowly. Manatees then have time to move out of the way.

endangered
at risk of dying out

Hands On: Warm Water Game

Manatees live best in water that is warmer than 70 degrees Fahrenheit (21 degrees Celsius). This game will show you how manatees must search for warm water.

What You Need

Four or more people
A swimming pool

What You Do

1. Choose one person to be the manatee searching for warm water. The other players should each choose a temperature between 60 and 80 degrees Fahrenheit (15 and 27 degrees Celsius). Do not tell anyone the temperature you have chosen.
2. Form a circle around the manatee.
3. The manatee swims up to one person in the circle. This person calls out his or her temperature.
4. If it is less than 70 degrees Fahrenheit (21 degrees Celsius), the manatee must swim to another person. If it is more than 70 degrees Fahrenheit (21 degrees Celsius), then the manatee can rest. The other player becomes the new manatee.

Manatees can die if they are in cold water for too long. They must search for warm water in the winter. Manatees sometimes swim as much as 500 miles (805 kilometers) to find water that is the right temperature.

Words to Know

herbivore (HUR-buh-vor)—an animal that eats mostly plants; manatees eat sea grass and other plants.

mammal (MAM-uhl)—a warm-blooded animal that has a backbone and feeds milk to its young; manatees are mammals.

mate (MATE)—to join together to produce young; manatees mate at any time during the year.

predator (PRED-uh-tur)—an animal that hunts and eats other animals

warm-blooded (warm-BLUHD-id)—having a body temperature that stays the same

Read More

Cole, Melissa S. *Manatee.* Wild Marine Animals! Woodbridge, Conn.: Blackbirch Press, 2001.

Klingel, Cynthia Fitterer, and Robert B. Noyed. *Manatees.* Wonder Books. Chanhassen, Minn.: Child's World, 2002.

Theodorou, Rod. *Florida Manatee.* Animals in Danger. Chicago: Heinemann Library, 2001.

Internet Sites

Kids Only: Manatees & Dugongs
http://www.cep.unep.org/kids/kids.html
Save the Manatee Club
http://www.savethemanatee.org

Index